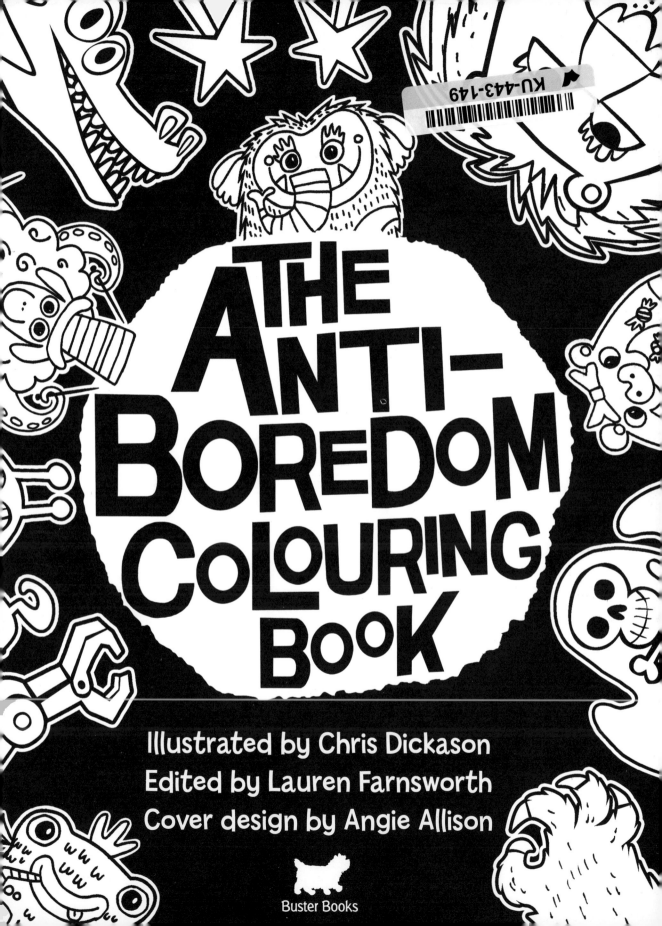

THE ANTI-BOREDOM COLOURING BOOK

Illustrated by Chris Dickason
Edited by Lauren Farnsworth
Cover design by Angie Allison

Buster Books

Leave boring old Planet Earth behind and blast off to a place called Planet Anti-Boredom.

It's a place where everything is barmy and bonkers. It's a place where crocodiles drive racing cars, dinosaurs graze with cows, and you can have your very own pet shark.

Grab your pens, colour in Planet Anti-Boredom and you'll never be bored again.

What is hiding
in the bedroom?

Boredom
multiplied.

It's raining food.

Please
DO
feed the
animals.

Drive away boredom.

Dare you to eat THIS.

It's a Kangaducklebat!

A day at the races ... and they're off!

Make sure your feet aren't bored.

Introducing the Anti-Boredom teachers ...

Monsieur de Gravy teaches Cookery.

Mr Digibotford teaches Maths.

Mr Old teaches History.

Sir Draggybopkins is the Headteacher.

Mr Mutant teaches Science.

Miss Lingoloo teaches English.

Mrs Bufftash teaches Games.

Time for a spot of gardening.

Feeding time for the fish.

Anti-Boredom - outside and in.

Boredom drives you loopy.

... bonkers!

Enjoy the wacky works of art.

Good night, sleep tight. Don't let boredom bite.

What flies in the skies on Planet Anti-Boredom?

A barbecue, Anti-Boredom style.

Go barmy on the beach.

Hairy, scary hamsters.

Escape to the crazy countryside.

Downside up.

You'll befriend some bizarre buddies.

Dancing dog.

Crazy cat.

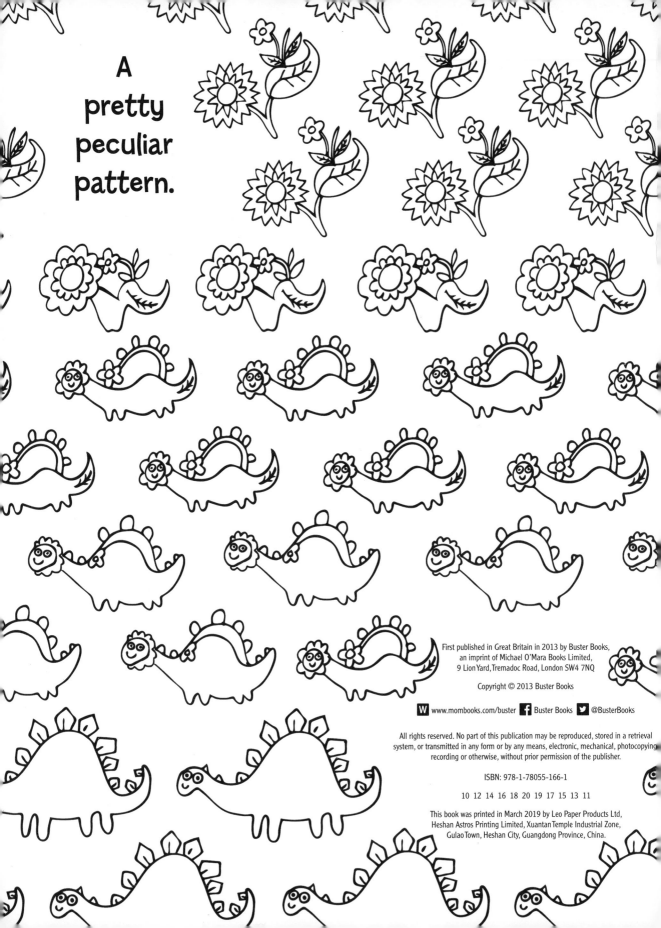

A pretty peculiar pattern.

First published in Great Britain in 2013 by Buster Books,
an imprint of Michael O'Mara Books Limited,
9 Lion Yard, Tremadoc Road, London SW4 7NQ

Copyright © 2013 Buster Books

W www.mombooks.com/buster F Buster Books Y @BusterBooks

ISBN: 978-1-78055-166-1

10 12 14 16 18 20 19 17 15 13 11

This book was printed in March 2019 by Leo Paper Products Ltd,
Heshan Astros Printing Limited, Xuantan Temple Industrial Zone,
Gulao Town, Heshan City, Guangdong Province, China.